LIVING WITH
DISORDERS AND
DISABILITIES

LIVING WITH

ADHD

by Whitney Sanderson

ReferencePoint
Press®

San Diego, CA

Content Consultant: Eric Lewkowiez, MD, Augusta University

LIBRARY OF CONGRESS CATALOGING-IN-PUBLICATION DATA

Name: Sanderson, Whitney, 1986– author.
Title: Living with ADHD / by Whitney Sanderson.
Description: San Diego, CA : ReferencePoint Press, Inc., [2019] | Series:
    Living with Disorders and Disabilities | Audience: Grade 9 to 12. |
    Includes bibliographical references and index.
Identifiers: LCCN 2018011536 (print) | LCCN 2018011759 (ebook) | ISBN
    9781682824801 (ebook) | ISBN 9781682824795 (hardback)
Subjects: LCSH: Attention-deficit hyperactivity disorder—Juvenile
    literature.
Classification: LCC RJ506.H9 (ebook) | LCC RJ506.H9 S267 2019 (print) | DDC
    618.92/8589—dc23
LC record available at https://lccn.loc.gov/2018011536

CONTENTS

THREE FACES OF ADHD

Fourteen-year-old Olivia carried the plate of freshly baked cookies to the kitchen table. Her friends were waiting with smiles on their faces. But as they bit into the cookies, their smiles faded. Her friend Jacklyn coughed, swallowed quickly, and took a sip of milk.

Olivia glanced at the recipe and then flushed. It called for a teaspoon of baking soda, but she recalled having used a cup of it instead. How could she have been so careless?

Her friends laughed. "Typical Olivia," said Grace. Olivia forced herself to laugh with them, but Grace's comment stung. After her friends went home, Olivia started thinking. How was it possible she could play *Minecraft* or run cross-country for hours with laser focus, but she couldn't follow a simple recipe? Lately, it seemed like anything she did turned into a disaster.

Inattentiveness is one of the hallmark symptoms of ADHD. People may have trouble focusing at school, work, and home.

Attention Problems

Tori pulled into her reserved parking space outside the high-rise office building—twenty minutes late. When she got to her desk, Tori sat down at her computer to find nearly one hundred emails waiting, many of them marked "urgent." Although she felt pulled in ten different directions, soon she was totally absorbed in her work. Before she knew it, she had worked right through the lunch meeting she had planned with her marketing manager. She dashed off an apology by email, saying that a client call had gone longer than expected. She didn't like lying, but that felt better than admitting she forgot.

On the Move

Art class was Aidan's favorite part of the day. His second-grade teacher had all the kids line up to get their trays of paint. Aidan spun in circles to distract himself while he waited his turn. As he drifted out of line, Carly cut in front of him and got the last new tray without dried-up paint crusted on it. Almost before he knew it, he pushed Carly to the floor and grabbed her tray.

The principal sent Aidan home from school early. At home, his mom sent him outside to play basketball to work off some of his energy. As Aidan shot baskets, his ball bounced down the driveway. He ran after it.

A horn blasted and tires screeched. Aidan looked up just as a delivery truck swerved off the road and onto the lawn. "You ran right in front of me!" shouted the driver as Aidan's mom came running from the house. She yelled at Aidan, too.

Aidan did not like to see his mom so upset. But this day ended the way many of his days ended, with him being sent to his room to think about what he had done. All he knew was that everyone seemed to be mad at him all the time, even when he was just being himself.

At first glance, Olivia, Tori, and Aidan don't seem to have much in common. But each of them is having trouble in his or her daily life for the same reason. They all have attention deficit hyperactivity disorder (ADHD), "a chronic condition marked by persistent inattention, hyperactivity, and sometimes impulsivity."[1] Their examples are fictional, but they illustrate the different symptoms people with ADHD often experience. Olivia struggles with inattentiveness and forgetfulness. Tori has problems with distractibility and impatience, and Aidan has problems with hyperactivity and self-control. As the National Institute of Mental Health explains, "Inattention and hyperactivity/impulsivity are the key behaviors of ADHD. Some people with ADHD only have problems with one of the behaviors, while others have both inattention and hyperactivity-impulsivity."[2] Although the causes of ADHD are not known with certainty, the editors of *ADDitude* magazine note, "What we do know is that ADHD is not caused by bad parenting, too much sugar, or too many video games. It is a brain-based, biological disorder."[3]

According to CHADD, a clearinghouse of information on ADHD, "ADHD is a real disorder with potentially devastating consequences when not properly identified, diagnosed, and treated."[4] Increased awareness of ADHD has led to both higher rates of diagnosis and greater treatment effectiveness in the last several decades. Help is available to assist people living with ADHD. As one person with ADHD writes, "If there's anything I've learned in recent years—it's that living with ADHD is more of a lifestyle factor rather than a 'mental disorder.'"[5] With proper diagnosis and treatment, Olivia, Tori, Aidan, and others like them can chart a positive course through life despite the challenges presented by ADHD.

> "Inattention and hyperactivity/impulsivity are the key behaviors of ADHD. Some people with ADHD only have problems with one of the behaviors, while others have both inattention and hyperactivity-impulsivity."[2]
>
> —*National Institute of Mental Health*

Chapter 1

WHAT IS ADHD?

Attention deficit hyperactivity disorder is a neurodevelopmental, or brain-based, condition that affects people's ability to focus their attention and control their behavior. The symptoms begin in childhood and are usually noticeable by age six or seven.

Teachers are often the first to notice signs of ADHD in a child. Parents might be aware that their child is unusually active or has difficulty paying attention, but they may be unsure if their child's behavior is within the normal range for the child's age. Once children enter school and have to sit still and concentrate for longer amounts of time, their symptoms are typically more obvious.

Children themselves often become aware in their early school years that they are different in some way. They may be disliked or bullied because their behavior annoys other students. They may have trouble navigating complex social dynamics with other students

Students with ADHD can have difficulty adhering to behavioral norms at school. They may talk or use their smartphones at inappropriate times.

or notice that they are not learning and remembering as easily as their classmates.

Blake Taylor, the author of the memoir *ADHD & Me,* was diagnosed at age five. He recalls that his babysitter once strapped him to a kitchen chair with a bungee cord in an effort to get him to sit still long enough to finish his dinner. He also saw that his behavior set him apart. "At school, kids avoided me and teased me," he writes. "So, in response, I started isolating myself from them. . . . I was regarded as different, and kids don't want to be friends with someone who seems unusual."[6]

Students often struggle academically, too, but not because they lack intelligence. Their difficulties stem more from an inability to concentrate and stay on task. Eliana Letzter, a young woman who struggles with severe ADHD, recalls, "I could see my classmates finishing the assignments in 10 to 30 minutes. But they'd take me hours and hours and hours and sometimes I couldn't complete them."[7]

Core Symptoms

ADHD has three core symptoms: inattentiveness, hyperactivity, and impulsivity.

Inattentiveness is an inability to keep one's focus on a task, conversation, or train of thought. People with ADHD may find their minds wander or jump from topic to topic. Problems with working memory—the portion of one's short-term memory that temporarily holds and processes information—are common in ADHD. Angelique Landy Borgmeyer, writing on the mental health advocacy website *The Mighty*, says,

> For me it is a constant struggle to remember—to remember what needs to be done next, what needs to come first, what I need to bring for an appointment, when an appointment is, what time I need to leave, what I have to make dinner with, when I need to pay a bill, and that's just one day. I can have a dozen color coded sticky notes on the walls and a whole variety of alerts and reminders on my phone, but as soon as I look away the thought has disappeared.[8]

Keeping track of time is another common difficulty. People with ADHD often feel their sense of time is distorted. Time either passes with torturous slowness, or it speeds by so fast that hours seem to pass in an instant. ADHD causes people to be easily sidetracked by sights, sounds, or other sensations from the surrounding environment. A student might find it impossible to tune out the noise of construction trucks outside her classroom, or she might find a friend's strong perfume so distracting that she misses what the friend is saying. Some people with ADHD feel like they are getting too much sensory input and don't know how to organize it. Mike Moon describes it this way for *The Mighty*: "My mind is in 100 different spots at once. Each of them seems equally important to get done and it seems like I have to get them done all at once. I bounce from one thing to another. My mind is in a fog that I can't clear. A thousand thoughts race through my head all at once."[9]

The second core symptom of ADHD, hyperactivity, is excessive physical activity that a person can't easily control. Many children have high energy, but kids with hyperactivity find it almost painful to sit still. Staying in their seats at school or in a waiting room requires an intense effort that they usually can't keep up for long. Even if they don't leave their seats, they might tap their hands or feet, shuffle papers, chew on a pencil, or find other ways of releasing their pent-up need for movement.

> "My mind is in 100 different spots at once. Each of them seems equally important to get done and it seems like I have to get them done all at once. I bounce from one thing to another. My mind is in a fog that I can't clear. A thousand thoughts race through my head all at once."[9]
>
> —Mike Moon, man with ADHD

Anna Selleck, describing her preschool-age son's hyperactivity, writes, "He climbed everything and ran around like a firecracker all day, usually with a little plastic hippopotamus in each hand. At nursery when I came to collect him, the other children would be sitting round for circle time. He would be clambering on the climbing frame, a plastic hippo tucked away in one sticky paw."[10]

Hyperactivity is usually more noticeable in children than in adults. As people with ADHD mature, they are better able to control their impulse to move around in situations where doing so would be inappropriate. But they may still feel restless, fidget, and make up excuses to get up as often as possible. As J. Russell Ramsay, professor of psychiatry, puts it, "You don't see ADHD adults in graduate school standing on their chairs. But the hyperactivity has just gone underground."[11]

The third core ADHD symptom, impulsivity, is a lack of ability to delay rewards or consider the consequences of an action before doing it. Children with ADHD may talk too much, interrupt others, or blurt out answers in class. Like Aidan, they sometimes do dangerous things such as running into the street before thinking about the risks. All children have trouble controlling their impulses, and they slowly build up this skill over time. That's why it's important for a mental health professional to determine whether a child's impulsive behavior is more pronounced than what is appropriate for his or her age.

"You don't see ADHD adults in graduate school standing on their chairs. But the hyperactivity has just gone underground."[11]

—J. Russell Ramsay, psychiatry professor

Impulsiveness can often put people with ADHD in dangerous situations. This risky behavior can be illegal or harmful.

Tammy Murphy, whose eleven-year-old son Joe has ADHD with impulsivity, once asked him why he had so much trouble considering the consequences of his actions. He replied, "Well, it's kind of like your heart beating. You do it, but you don't even know it's happening."[12]

Teens and adults with impulsivity may see themselves as "adrenaline junkies," seeking out high-risk jobs, extreme sports, and even criminal activity. People with ADHD can also be verbally impulsive, saying things that damage their relationships or careers. Impulsivity can also show up as frequent changes in jobs or snap decisions to quit school. Adults sometimes struggle with impulsive spending that leads to debt and financial instability, as well as unpredictable behavior that harms their relationships.

ADHD Incidence

In 1994, the American Psychiatric Association estimated that 3 to 5 percent of elementary school children had ADHD. The prevalence of ADHD diagnoses has increased since then. According to 2013–2015 data from the Centers for Disease Control and Prevention, 10.4 percent of children aged five to seventeen have ever been diagnosed with ADHD. One possible reason for the increase since 1994 is that greater awareness of ADHD has caused more parents to seek diagnosis and treatment for their children. Some mental health professionals believe ADHD is now overdiagnosed, especially in young boys. Other professionals believe many cases are still missed, especially in girls and in older adults who grew up before the diagnosis of ADHD existed.

People with ADHD can have each of the core symptoms to different degrees. Hyperactivity and impulsivity often appear together, and some people only have problems with inattention. People who have mainly attention problems sometimes describe themselves as having "attention deficit disorder," or ADD. However, the official name for all types of the disorder is ADHD, whether hyperactivity is present or not. Olivia, who struggles with keeping track of details and managing her attention, has inattentive-type ADHD. Tori experiences both inattentiveness and impulsivity, and Aidan demonstrates inattentive, impulsive, and hyperactive behavior.

Because of the wide range of symptoms, the behavior of people with ADHD can look very different from one person to the next. Jessica McCabe, who runs an educational YouTube channel called *How to ADHD*, says, "If you've met one person with ADHD, you've met *one person* with ADHD."[13] People of all ages, cultures, personality types, IQs, and levels of education can have ADHD. Boys are diagnosed about twice as often as girls. Recent figures indicate that 14.2 percent of boys aged five to seventeen have ever been diagnosed with ADHD, compared to 6.4 percent of girls. The condition often co-occurs with mental health conditions such as anxiety, depression, and learning disabilities. Co-occurrence can make diagnosis and treatment more complicated.

Lifelong Disorder?

Mental health professionals used to believe children with ADHD would outgrow it by late adolescence. Research from the last several decades tells a different story. Studies show that some children do improve until they have few or no ADHD symptoms, but more than half will continue to have ADHD as adults. Adults simply have the benefit of having had more years in which to learn how to manage and mask their symptoms. Approximately 11 percent of children aged four to seventeen and 8 percent of adults in the United States have been diagnosed with ADHD.

CEO of the Brain

The symptoms of ADHD are caused by problems with a cognitive process called executive functioning. Executive functioning takes place in the prefrontal cortex of the brain, the area just behind the forehead that is often called the "CEO of the brain." Just like the chief executive of a company, the prefrontal cortex makes decisions based on many sources of information—in this case, the input comes from other areas of the brain.

At every waking moment, we all form thoughts based on input from our senses, emotions, and memories. Making sense of these various inputs enables us to make predictions about the future. In a split second, we must use executive functioning to sort all this information, weigh its importance, and decide on what action to take as a result. Then, we have to plan the action, organize it, and carry it out. If we get new information at any point, we might have to revise our plan. When this complicated process does not work smoothly, a person's behavior will seem disorganized. ADHD can cause serious problems in school, work, and relationships. People who have it are more likely to drop out of high school or college, abuse drugs and alcohol, be fired from a job, or end up in jail.

Living with the ADHD Label

Clinical psychologist Russell Barkley emphasizes the potentially serious consequences of having ADHD. "As adults, people with ADHD are five times more likely to speed and three times more likely to have their licenses revoked than other people. They're more likely to experience accidental injuries—burns, poisoning, traffic accidents, all kinds of trauma—than other people. In fact, having ADHD makes you three times more likely to be dead by the age of 45."[14]

> "As adults, people with ADHD are five times more likely to speed and three times more likely to have their licenses revoked than other people."[14]
>
> —Clinical psychologist Russell Barkley

People with ADHD may be reluctant to tell others they have it. Many psychiatric conditions carry a stigma—negative judgments that cause feelings of shame and isolation—and ADHD is no exception. Jessica McCabe describes the effect as "little emotional wounds from being judged by the outside world—or ourselves!"[15] People with ADHD often struggle with the belief that they are lazy, unmotivated, or unintelligent. Sometimes these judgments are self-imposed, and sometimes they come from others.

People with ADHD often report that friends, family members, or coworkers do not take the condition seriously. It can be frustrating when a person who does not have ADHD says he is "having an ADHD moment" because he lost his car keys, or jokes that a child having a tantrum in public needs Ritalin (a medication often prescribed to treat ADHD). People who have ADHD may feel annoyed when their condition is used as a joke or when people don't understand that ADHD is more consequential than being a little scatterbrained.

There are also people, even a few medical experts, who claim ADHD does not exist. They may argue that the disorder exists to enrich drug companies, or that ADHD is just a way of describing normal childhood energy as a disease. Psychologist Keith Conners, who created a well-known rating scale for ADHD, counters this claim, responding: "Take one of these kids on a car trip for a day and see how you feel about it then."[16]

Even people who are trying to be supportive may not fully understand ADHD. Kathleen O'Brien, a college student, has heard some variation of, "you're too smart to have ADHD" more times than she can count. "When they tell me I'm lazy or tell me to just focus they don't see how much it hurts. They don't see that I am already beating myself up on the inside," she writes. "They don't see me yelling at my brain to just read the darn page and stop listening to the girl tapping her shoe. They don't see me wishing I could just be like everyone else who can go out on a Saturday because they finished their homework already."[17]

Hearing their symptoms described as laziness, naughtiness, or lack of intelligence can be especially harmful to children, who are building up a concept of themselves and their abilities. Researcher Stephen Hinshaw says, "I've gotten to know hundreds of children who have ADHD, and I've heard many say things like, 'I just can't make it,' or 'I'm just not cut out for school.' The stigma has so corrupted their motivation that they've given up even trying to be successful."[18]

The Gifts of ADHD

On the other hand, many people with ADHD say it has a positive side, too. The condition is often associated with high energy levels, creativity, and an ability to generate innovative ideas. Research supports these observations. A study by Holly White and Priti Shah found that people with ADHD scored higher on a measure of divergent thinking, or the ability to come up with original ideas and solutions. Bonnie Cramond, a researcher and expert on giftedness, has found several traits of highly creative people that overlap with ADHD. Among these are spontaneous idea generation, mind wandering, daydreaming, sensation seeking, energy, and impulsivity—a mix of what most people would think of as positive and negative traits.

Given their typical difficulty in focusing on a task, it is somewhat surprising that many people with ADHD can hyperfocus, or concentrate deeply on something that really interests them. Rebecca Winchell, a recent college graduate with ADHD, describes hyperfocus as "a state of intense, single-minded concentration on one particular thing, to the point that you might become oblivious to everything else around you. You might lose track of time, or forget about chores, deadlines, and other obligations because you are so focused on this one thing."[19] It may be hard to get someone's attention if she is in this state, and she may feel annoyed or disoriented when interrupted. Unfortunately for people with ADHD, hyperfocus is not a quality that is easily tamed. Just because someone wants to finish a school assignment or a work project doesn't mean he will be able to hyperfocus on it. Often, people with ADHD can channel hyperfocus only in an area of natural talent or interest, such as a playing a favorite game, sport, or instrument.

Gymnast Simone Biles is one well-known person with ADHD. She has spoken out in the media about the disorder.

Some people with ADHD have used their way of thinking and learning to build highly successful careers. There seems to be a link between entrepreneurship and ADHD, perhaps because the high-risk/high-reward scenario of starting a business attracts people with these traits. JetBlue Airways founder David Neeleman says, "I struggled a lot in school. I really had a hard time with standardized tests, staying focused and absorbing information from a written page into my brain. It was tough. I thought I was stupid, that I didn't have what the other kids had. In third grade, sitting inside at recess, not being able to go out, because I couldn't get my work done."[20]

Neeleman later discovered his problems were caused by ADHD. The condition didn't stop him from founding a total of four commercial airlines worth hundreds of millions of dollars. But despite his success, he still struggles with basic activities, such as putting his socks in the laundry basket instead of on the floor (an example he says his wife is fond of giving). Neeleman created the first e-ticketing system, now used in every airport, to solve a problem caused by his ADHD: he kept losing his boarding pass before taking flights. He writes, "With the disorganization, procrastination and inability to focus, and all the other bad things that come with ADHD, there also come creativity and the ability to take risks." He adds, "If someone told me you could be normal or you could continue to have your ADHD, I would take ADHD."[21]

Other headline-grabbing people with ADHD include comedian Jim Carrey, Grammy Award–winning singer Justin Timberlake, Olympic gymnast Simone Biles, former Pittsburgh Steelers quarterback Terry Bradshaw, Pulitzer Prize–winning journalist Katherine Ellison, and chef Jamie Oliver.

> "If someone told me you could be normal or you could continue to have your ADHD, I would take ADHD."[21]
>
> —David Neeleman, JetBlue Airways founder

One of the most respected experts in the field of ADHD research, psychiatrist Edward Hallowell, has ADHD and dyslexia himself. He says, "In my work as a psychiatrist who treats ADHD, I see myself not as a doctor who treats a disability, but rather as a doctor who helps people, adults and children alike, identify, develop, and celebrate their talents."[22] One person he helped was Neeleman, whom Hallowell diagnosed with ADHD. For Neeleman and many people with ADHD, getting diagnosed was a turning point that helped them understand how their brains work and how they can put them to best use.

Chapter 2

ADHD SYMPTOMS AND DIAGNOSIS

In 1798, Scottish physician Sir Alexander Crichton first wrote about a disorder similar to ADHD. He described it as "the incapacity of attending with a necessary degree of constancy to any one object . . . by which means this faculty [attention] is incessantly withdrawn from one impression to another. It may be either born with a person or it may be the effect of accidental diseases."[23]

Although the language Crichton used is different from modern ways of talking about ADHD, he clearly described an inability to focus that is one of the key indicators of ADHD. In 1844, German doctor Heinrich Hoffman wrote a poem describing a young boy whose hyperactive behavior caused trouble at the dinner table. The poem, containing the lines "Fidgety Phil, he won't sit still," was a Christmas present for Hoffman's three-year-old son (perhaps the inspiration for the poem?), but it was a hit among his medical colleagues, too. The poem was translated into English and published in the British medical journal *The Lancet* in 1904.

In 1934, two Yale University researchers, Eugen Kahn and Louis Cohen, described people with a condition they called "organic drivenness." Their findings were based on observations of people who had contracted encephalitis during the epidemic of 1917 to 1928. These subjects exhibited behavioral symptoms such as hyperactivity, impulsiveness, and poor attention spans. Kahn and Cohen concluded these symptoms had to have a medical cause—perhaps low-level inflammation of the brain, which tests of that era couldn't detect.

About the same time, in 1932, physician Charles Bradley became the director of a Rhode Island hospital for children with neurological disorders or learning and behavioral problems. He discovered by accident that Benzedrine, a stimulant drug used to treat headaches, improved the behavior and school performance of about one-half of the children with behavioral disorders who took the drug. This finding was surprising in that a stimulant drug would be expected to increase hyperactivity, not lessen it.

In the late 1950s, researchers continued to pursue a link between the brain and behavior, and the condition now known as ADHD came to be called "minimal brain dysfunction." By the 1960s, Benzedrine and similar drugs known as methylphenidates, such as Ritalin, were often used to treat hyperactive children. In 1968, the first mention of an ADHD-like disorder, "hyperkinetic reaction of childhood," appeared

ADHD and the *DSM-5*

The *DSM-5* is the fifth edition of a manual published by the American Psychiatric Association containing diagnostic criteria for every mental disorder. The *DSM* was first published in 1952, and every new edition is compiled by a task force of experts who review the criteria for each diagnosis. With each updated version, some conditions are dropped and others are added. Names and descriptions of conditions and information about their prevalence also change over time.

The *DSM-5* has become increasingly important as more people use health insurance to pay for mental health treatment. Before insurance companies will pay for medication or therapy, they require clinicians to submit a diagnosis from the *DSM-5* or the *International Classification of Diseases* (*ICD-10*), a manual that contains information about every medical condition.

Many mental health professionals argue that this emphasis on diagnostic labels leads to an incomplete understanding of clients and a lack of personalized treatment. The benefit of the *DSM-5* is that when ADHD is discussed among mental health professionals, they know they are talking about the same set of symptoms. Good clinicians use a confirmed ADHD diagnosis as a starting point, but they make an effort to understand their client as a complete, complex person.

in the second edition of the *Diagnostic and Statistical Manual of Mental Disorders* (*DSM*).

Two years later, Canadian psychologist Virginia Douglas discovered that problems with attention often went along with hyperactive behavior, and that some children seemed to have mostly attention problems without hyperactivity. Experts were beginning to put together the fact that both the children who ran around and disrupted their classmates and the children who stared quietly out the window had the same brain-based condition.

In 1980, the diagnosis of "Attention Deficit Disorder, with or without hyperactivity" first appeared in the *DSM*. Then in 1987, the hyperactivity distinction was removed, and all forms of the condition came to be called attention deficit hyperactivity disorder. That term is still in use today, though three subtypes were identified in *DSM*'s 2000 edition: combined type ADHD, predominantly inattentive type ADHD, and predominantly hyperactive-impulsive ADHD. In the 2013 edition (*DSM-5*), the types became known as combined presentation, predominantly hyperactive/impulsive presentation, and predominantly inattentive presentation.

ADHD terminology can be confusing, and the many names for the condition show how the medical community's understanding of it has changed over time. In the future, ADHD may come to be known by yet a different name. Some experts, such as Barkley, suggest that descriptive terms such as "self-regulation-deficit disorder" or "executive functioning disorder" would be more accurate than the current terminology.

Brain Imaging

In 1982, a General Electric scientist, John Schenck, volunteered to be the test subject for some cutting-edge technology that he had been working on. As Schenck lay motionless on a table, a giant magnet interacted with water molecules in his brain. The magnetic field produced a picture that was transmitted to a computer screen nearby. This magnetic resonance imaging (MRI) scan was the first time an image of a living person's brain had been recorded, and it changed neurology research forever. Instead of just having theories about brain differences, scientists could see the physical variations.

In the last several decades, advances in brain-imaging technology have allowed scientists to observe the structure and functioning of the brain even more clearly. One of the most useful types of brain imaging

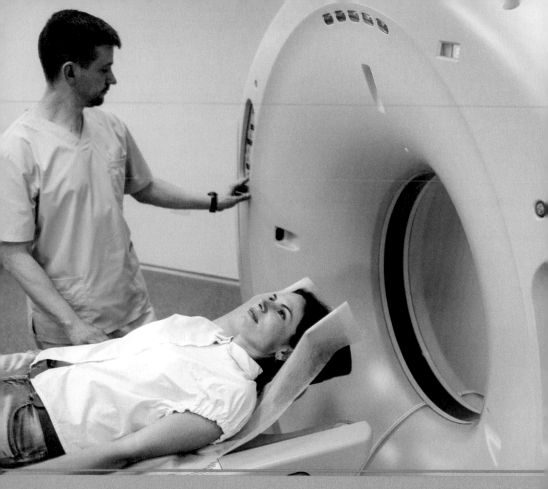

The advent of magnetic resonance imaging has opened up many avenues of research. This technology gives doctors an unprecedented look into the brain.

for studying ADHD is called functional magnetic resonance imaging, or fMRI. This technology allows researchers to see changes in blood flow, which is a sign of brain activity, to different areas of the brain.

All parts of the brain have receptors for many different neurotransmitters, which are chemicals that are made within the brain. One neurotransmitter, dopamine, seems to be involved in ADHD. Dopamine is the brain's chemical reward signal. When it is released into synapses, or spaces between nerve cells, it produces feelings of pleasure, motivation, and focus. Low levels of dopamine can cause feelings of depression, irritability, restlessness, or tiredness. Very high levels can cause restlessness, paranoia, and hallucinations. In people with ADHD, dopamine does not reach the right areas of the brain in the right amounts. Other neurochemicals, such as norepinephrine and serotonin, may also be affected. So far, fMRI research has identified at least four areas of the brain that appear to be underactive in people with ADHD:

- The prefrontal cortex, which is involved in decision-making, organizing information, and other tasks of executive functioning;

- The limbic system, which is involved in processing emotions;

- The basal ganglia, which act like a "control center" for the brain by sending sensory information to different areas; and

- The reticular activating system, which is an area that controls attention and motivation.

Most ADHD medications work by increasing the release of dopamine and raising the level of norepinephrine. People without ADHD who have normal levels of dopamine will sometimes feel excited and "speedy" if they take this type of medication. But people with ADHD often feel more calm and focused. This is probably because the medication is raising their dopamine levels from being too low to normal, causing their prefrontal cortex to become more active.

ADHD and the Family

In the past, experts believed that bad parenting caused brain disorders such as schizophrenia or autism. While this theory has since been discredited, it serves as an example of how parents have historically been blamed for the behavior of their children. Researchers now know that brain function is often at the root of many behavioral issues. Although it is true that children who have experienced abuse or other traumas are more likely to be diagnosed with ADHD, the everyday choices most parents make will not put a child any more or less at risk.

ADHD does seem to run in families. Researchers have identified a number of genes that make people more likely to have ADHD. For any child with ADHD, there is up to a 50 percent chance that a parent has it, too. Growing up in a household where both a parent and one or more children have ADHD can be an exercise in controlled chaos. Katherine Ellison, a Pulitzer Prize–winning journalist whose son Buzz, like her, also has ADHD, describes "a terrible fight that we had while I was driving down the highway with two of my kids in the car, and they were fighting, and I had the radio on, and we were late, and I was thinking about everything that I needed to do that day plus the fact that the stock market was down 300 points and the Himalayan glaciers were retreating."[24] On the brink of sending Buzz to boarding school, Ellison took a year to research ADHD and wrote a memoir, *Buzz: A Year of Paying Attention*, about the different treatment options they tried. In the end, she found medication helped both Buzz and her, but she considers the time and attention she was able to give Buzz the most important factor in improving their relationship.

Gender and ADHD

When people imagine someone with ADHD, they often think of a young, hyperactive boy. Statistically, they're right. Girls are more likely to have inattentive-type ADHD, while boys are more likely to have hyperactive and impulsive symptoms. The reason is probably

Family relations can be strained when one or more members have ADHD. Teens may feel distant from their parents.

a mix of biology and social conditioning. Boys are usually expected to be active and bold, while girls are expected to be quiet and cooperative. However, there are also plenty of distractible, quiet boys with ADHD and lots of loud, on-the-go girls. Life can sometimes be hard for children who defy gender norms as they also struggle with ADHD symptoms.

Each gender faces unique challenges with ADHD. Boys with the condition are more likely to be labeled as troublemakers. They might assume the role of class clown or class bully to shield themselves from the pain of being different. But beneath their rough and rowdy exterior, boys with ADHD also want to be liked and included by others. Physician Larry Silver writes that it is especially important for boys to have strong male role models who can help them build social skills, focus their energy on positive goals, and develop self-control. Says Silver, "[Boys] need to learn how to cope and to compensate. They may need to use medication and other forms of help. They must sense that their dad understands and supports all that is being done. If dad does not accept them as they are, how can they accept themselves?"[25]

While boys with ADHD often stand out, girls all too often blend in. Girls with inattentive ADHD might not get diagnosed, because they keep to themselves in the classroom. They don't cause trouble, but they also aren't able to live up to their potential. As teenagers, girls with ADHD may have trouble paying attention to social cues that indicate they are in dangerous situations. They are at higher risk for unwanted pregnancies and sexual assault. Because hyperactive behavior is seen more often in boys, girls with this type

"[Boys] need to learn how to cope and to compensate. They may need to use medication and other forms of help. They must sense that their dad understands and supports all that is being done. If dad does not accept them as they are, how can they accept themselves?"[25]

—Larry Silver, physician

of ADHD may face rejection from both teachers and classmates who feel they aren't living up to the way girls "should" act. Jay Salpekar, a child psychiatrist who runs an ADHD clinic in Washington, DC, believes sports are especially helpful for girls with ADHD so they can channel their energy in a socially accepted way. Says Salpekar, "Sports offer lots of social interaction in addition to physical fitness, and it helps get them out of their shell."[26]

> **"Sports offer lots of social interaction in addition to physical fitness, and it helps get [girls] out of their shell."[26]**
>
> —Jay Salpekar, child psychiatrist

ADHD Professionals

Only qualified professionals can make a diagnosis of ADHD. These include psychiatrists, physicians in other specialties, clinical psychologists, and neuropsychologists (practitioners with a PhD degree who test for brain-based conditions). Other types of non–mental health professionals, such as life coaches, naturopathic doctors, acupuncturists, and physical therapists cannot diagnose ADHD, although they may offer supportive treatments. People who suspect they have ADHD should consult with a qualified and experienced professional.

Licensed physicians are the only practitioners who can prescribe medication for ADHD. In some states, a licensed psychiatric nurse or physician assistant, working in a practice overseen by a medical doctor, can also prescribe medication. A number of other mental health professionals can provide talk-based therapy for clients with ADHD. These include clinical psychologists; school psychologists and

A wide range of health professionals can offer support to people affected by ADHD. Talk therapy is one useful method for treating the disorder.

educational psychologists; licensed social workers; licensed mental health counselors; and licensed marriage and family therapists.

Many people suspect they have ADHD before they get an official diagnosis. They might find a list of *DSM* criteria online, read articles about the condition, take an online quiz, or receive input from family and friends. Their instincts are often accurate, but it is important that they seek a professional diagnosis—both to rule out other conditions that can look like ADHD and to get pointed in the direction of proper treatment.

First Step: Diagnosis

The first time someone meets with a professional about ADHD-related concerns, he or she will undergo what is called an intake or diagnostic interview. During this time, the clinician will ask detailed questions about the symptoms that prompted concerns. The clinician will also obtain background information about the person's family, medical history, school or work performance, and any past traumas or other important life experiences.

Along with obtaining factual information, the clinician will carefully observe the person seeking treatment, noting facial expression, tone of voice, body language, clothing and appearance, manner of speaking, and apparent mood. The clinician will notice if the person seems confused or disoriented, or whether he seems to be having difficulty expressing himself or is experiencing intense emotions.

Depending on the severity of a person's ADHD, symptoms can be almost invisible to others or they can be obvious. A clinician might notice a client fidgeting in her seat, forgetting the clinician's name, showing up late to the appointment, jumping from topic to topic, or frequently losing her train of thought.

When seeing children, clinicians nearly always seek information from parents, other family members, and teachers. Some clinicians will invite adult clients to bring a family member or partner to a session to get their perspective on the difficulties the person is having. This is especially helpful if the client lacks self-awareness about how her behavior is affecting others.

Professionals use guidelines from the *DSM* to diagnose any mental health condition. The most recent edition, *DSM-5,* states that symptoms of ADHD must begin before a child is twelve years old. To be diagnosed with inattentive ADHD, a child must meet six of nine criteria, and anyone being diagnosed over age seventeen must meet five of them. The criteria concern issues such as paying attention to details, listening when spoken to, organizing and following through on tasks, losing personal items, and being easily distracted.

To be diagnosed with hyperactive/impulsive ADHD, a child must meet six of nine criteria, and anyone over seventeen must meet five. These include fidgeting or tapping, moving around when it is not appropriate, interrupting or talking excessively, having trouble waiting for a turn, and acting as if "driven by a motor."

An ADHD diagnosis is only given if a child or adult has had the symptoms for at least six months, and the symptoms are serious enough that they cause significant difficulty in daily life activities. ADHD can be classified as mild, moderate, or severe depending on how much difficulty with daily activities or risk of harm the symptoms cause.

In addition to observation and verbal interaction, clinicians typically use tools to measure ADHD symptoms, such as the Conners Comprehensive Behavior Rating Scales for children. The Conners tool comprises three questionnaires: one for parents, one for teachers, and one for the child. The questions differ on each form. For example, a question from the parent form is, "How often does your child have trouble going to sleep at night?" A question from the child form is, "How hard is it to focus on a homework assignment?" The clinician tabulates all the answers to arrive at a score. Higher scores mean there is a greater likelihood that the child has ADHD.

Although ADHD is typically diagnosed by behavioral observation, a type of electroencephalography (EEG) was approved by the Food and Drug Administration in 2013 as a tool to diagnose ADHD. Electroencephalography measures electrical patterns in the brain, typically referred to as brainwaves. Scientists have known that people with ADHD have a higher ratio of two kinds of brainwaves than do people without the condition. Quantitative electroencephalography (qEEG) enables digital analysis of these brainwaves. At present, qEEG is not widely used as a diagnostic tool, partly because many insurers are unwilling to pay for it.

Ruling Out Other Conditions

People are complex, and so are neurological disorders. Making a correct diagnosis is not always easy. A good clinician will make a thorough assessment of symptoms. For example, if an adult describes a child standing up from her desk and walking to the window every five minutes, this might seem like hyperactivity. But if the child says she does this because she feels something bad will happen otherwise, the practitioner might make a diagnosis of obsessive-compulsive disorder (OCD) instead of ADHD. One of the key symptoms of OCD is the need to repeat a specific action to reduce anxiety.

In the *DSM-5*, each disorder is accompanied by a list of several other conditions whose symptoms are similar to it. Sometimes people have ADHD plus one or more other conditions, so clinicians must carefully assess coexisting symptoms. Conditions with ADHD-like symptoms include:

- Pervasive developmental disorder, a condition that affects thinking and reasoning beyond what is seen in ADHD;

- Conduct disorder, which causes difficulty following social rules and respecting the rights of others;

- Depression, which can interfere with focus and motivation;

- Bipolar disorder, which causes shifts between depression and extreme excitability that can be confused with hyperactive/impulsive ADHD; and

- Anxiety disorders, which can cause problems with focus, memory, and sitting still.

Being diagnosed with ADHD can bring a wide range of reactions. People may feel relieved that their problem has a name, ashamed that they have a psychiatric disorder, fearful that ADHD may hold them back in life, sad that they had to struggle for so long, or angry that their condition was not diagnosed sooner. In an article for *ADDitude* magazine, reader Cherese writes, "Part of me was relieved to finally have a name for my symptoms, and part of me was upset because nobody wants to have anything 'wrong' with her."[27]

Many people find that receiving an ADHD diagnosis after years of struggling brings them hope. *ADDitude* reader Clare writes, "I will never let someone humiliate or put me down again. That happened all through school, and it was terrible. I was hard on myself at work before my [ADHD] diagnosis. Now I understand better what my deficits are, and I develop strategies and get the right supports in place to be successful. It has been a big shift in my life."[28]

Parents of children with ADHD often feel overwhelmed when their child receives an ADHD diagnosis. One parent, Mary, writes that her first reaction was to think, "'What do we do now?' We were unsure what the future would be like for our son. We pulled away from our friends who had children the same age, because our child could not compete with them (or so we thought). It is hard to put into words what parents feel when their child is diagnosed with a disability."[29]

Dan, a father of a child with ADHD, writes, "We worried. We didn't know anything about ADHD when our son was diagnosed. Our perception of attention deficit was mostly wrong. The diagnosis forced us to learn more about the condition, and that made us better parents."[30]

A child's ADHD diagnosis sometimes brings awareness that one or both parents have ADHD, too. When parents read the behavioral criteria for diagnosing ADHD, they may realize they fit the description themselves. Says Monica, the parent of a child who was diagnosed with ADHD, "When my child was diagnosed, I was relieved. It was also a clue that I might have the same problem. I went to the doctor and found out that I was correct."[31] In such cases, parents can explore treatment options for themselves and their children at the same time.

The effects of a diagnosis can be far-reaching. Michelle Beckett, who was diagnosed with ADHD as an adult, writes, "I truly believe that not only did this decision transform my life, but possibly saved it. The diagnosis itself lifted most of the guilt. Finally, an explanation. Not an excuse. My whole life made complete sense."[32]

> "I truly believe that not only did this decision transform my life, but possibly saved it. The diagnosis itself lifted most of the guilt. Finally, an explanation. Not an excuse. My whole life made complete sense."[32]
>
> —*Michelle Beckett, diagnosed with ADHD as an adult*

But obtaining an ADHD diagnosis from a qualified professional is only the beginning. The next step is to figure out what form of treatment is likely to be most helpful.

Chapter 3

LIVING WITH ADHD

ADHD affects people in all aspects of their lives. Some people have the most trouble at school or work, while others find social situations more challenging. But for many people with ADHD, school is the first place where their ADHD symptoms interfere with their daily activities in a significant way.

School

It is no coincidence that many children who are diagnosed with ADHD receive that diagnosis only after beginning their formal education. At school, students spend most of the day using skills that people with ADHD struggle with the most. These include focused attention, sitting quietly for long periods, and following a schedule. In the higher grades, students are also tasked with note-taking, remembering and recalling facts, and organizing information and thoughts into essays.

School accommodations are important in helping students with ADHD learn in a way that works for them. Even small adjustments can help improve their learning experience.

Some students who have ADHD or other mental or physical conditions have an IEP, or individualized education plan. This plan features modifications to the school day designed to help a child learn. For example, a student might be allowed to take a test in a quiet room instead of with other students or hold a stress ball during class. Some teachers make an extra effort to let children with ADHD be active, such as having them run errands within the building or sit on a balance ball instead of on a chair.

As many as half of people with ADHD also have specific learning disabilities such as dyslexia (difficulty with reading), dyscalculia (difficulty with math), and nonverbal learning disabilities (difficulty with social cues). ADHD medication does not treat these conditions, so it is important that children with ADHD be tested for other learning difficulties if any are suspected.

Most students with ADHD can function satisfactorily within a regular classroom. For students with severe ADHD, therapeutic residential schools with staff who specialize in teaching children with learning differences can be an appropriate solution. Eagle Hill School in Hardwick, Massachusetts, serves students in grades eight to twelve who have ADHD or learning disabilities. Eagle Hill is especially well known for its STAR program, in which professional artists and musicians spend a semester living on campus to mentor students. At Eagle Hill and in programs like it, students can engage in learning that is based in movement, art, emotion, and dance, teaching them that there are many paths to success outside of a traditional classroom.

Work

The transition from school to the workplace is often difficult for people with ADHD. As challenging as an academic environment can be, the built-in structure keeps many students on track. But once people get jobs, they are expected to work independently, solve problems on their own, and organize their own schedules. Ideally, they can channel their capacity for hyperfocusing into their work. But many people with ADHD feel overwhelmed, bored, or stuck in their jobs.

People with inattentive ADHD may not fully process instructions or may fail to remember important tasks. Those with hyperactive or impulsive ADHD may have conflicts with bosses and coworkers, send emails impulsively, or turn in projects without carefully checking their work. Adults with ADHD are more likely to experience unemployment,

ADHD can bring challenges in the workplace. Difficulty concentrating can reduce a worker's productivity.

and they earn an average of $5,000 to $10,000 per year less than colleagues who have the same education and experience.

Although laws in schools and workplaces protect people with disabilities, including ADHD, some employers may be reluctant to hire or retain a person with a condition that could affect his or her productivity. Psychologist Maelisa Hall recommends that her clients not focus on their diagnosis when requesting accommodations at work, but instead be straightforward and specific about what they need. For example, they could tell their boss, "I really need to reduce my distractions so I can focus on completing this project. I'm going to spend the next two hours in the conference room rather than in my noisy cubicle."[33] Enlisting the assistance of a coach can be especially helpful in navigating ADHD challenges related to work. For some

Hard Work Pays Off

One example of an ADHD success story is US Olympian Michelle Carter. At the 2016 Rio Olympics, Carter became the first US woman to win a gold medal in shot put. Carter, who perfected her skills while a student at the University of Texas, knows she presented challenges for her teachers as a young student. "I was definitely a handful back then," she notes. "I could not sit down long enough to study and to learn."[1] Fortunately for Carter, she was evaluated for her learning challenges early on. After being diagnosed with both ADHD and dyslexia, she was tutored several times a week and was able to succeed in school.

Since winning a gold medal, Carter has been an advocate for children with learning differences. One of her core messages is that people with ADHD can succeed at difficult tasks. "What I would tell a kid with ADHD and dyslexia or someone who struggles with anything in life is this: 'When you put your mind to it, you can do anything. . . . You may have to work a little bit harder, it may take a long time, you just may do it differently—but you can do it.'"[2]

1. Geri Coleman Tucker, "Chasing Gold, Olympic Shot Putter Michelle Carter Opens Up about ADHD and Dyslexia," *Understood*, July 28, 2016. www.understood.org.

2. Aimee Crawford, "Bravo, Simone Biles, for Taking a Stand Against ADHD Stigma," *ESPNW*, September 21, 2016. www.espn.com.

people, simple strategies such as keeping a to-do list or using a time management app can help them stay on track and be productive during the workday.

Everyday Activities

School and work encompass only a portion of the challenges and responsibilities people with ADHD face during the average day. Students have to manage homework, extracurricular activities, household chores, and possibly a part-time job once their school day ends. Adults' after-work responsibilities may include childcare, cooking, house cleaning, errands, and appointments. For many people with ADHD, staying focused at work or school requires so much effort that their mental and emotional reserves are depleted by the time they get home. Fatigue can then make it harder to exercise the self-control needed to get along with family members. Many experts recommend developing a consistent routine for mornings and evenings to minimize the number of decisions that need to be made. Children, as well as some adults, can benefit from visual reminders such as words or drawings on a whiteboard.

Judith Kolberg, a life coach, offers many tips to help people with ADHD be more organized at home. These include setting a time limit for making an important decision, setting a timer to avoid being hyperfocused on one task at the expense of others, and storing commonly used items in the same place all the time. Beth Main, a therapist and the founder of ADHD Solutions, says, "Don't rely on your memory; rely on good tools. . . . My motto is, 'If it's not on my calendar or to-do list, it's not going to happen.'"[34]

People with ADHD rarely have trouble focusing on hobbies they really enjoy. They are more likely to have trouble directing their attention away from these things, finding that they spent more time drawing, skateboarding, or playing video games than they intended. On the other hand, some people are quick to take up new hobbies or sports, only to lose interest when the novelty is gone. "The busy ADHD mind has a great capacity for dabbling in a variety of activities, and not going deep in any one area," says learning specialist and academic coach Theresa Maitland.[35] Maitland

> "The busy ADHD mind has a great capacity for dabbling in a variety of activities, and not going deep in any one area."[35]
>
> —*Theresa Maitland, learning specialist*

believes it is important for people to try a variety of activities, but also to cultivate the skill of sticking with something they truly enjoy.

Social Life

Making friends can be challenging for children, and this can be especially true for children with ADHD. In an article for *Time* magazine, journalist Denise Foley writes:

> *While kids with ADHD can be gregarious, their impulsiveness can create problems, often alienating others, including siblings, teachers, and classmates. They don't wait their turn, interrupt others, are easily frustrated, take wild risks, and their emotions can spill over like water at a rolling boil: They may be hot-headed, lash out violently, or have temper tantrums. All of this carries enormous social cost in school and on the playground.*[36]

For adults and children alike, many ingredients go into establishing a friendship. First is having fun together. People with ADHD, many of whom are creative and spontaneous, can be a lot of fun to be around. Another key element is consistency, which presents a struggle for many people with ADHD. Friends are expected to show up on time, remember important dates and events, keep secrets and confidences, and listen

"While kids with ADHD can be gregarious, their impulsiveness can create problems, often alienating others, including siblings, teachers, and classmates. . . . All of this carries enormous social cost in school and on the playground."[36]

—Denise Foley, journalist

carefully in conversations. Without these qualities, the other person might feel the person with ADHD is not truly invested in the friendship. In addition, since people with ADHD may find it too overwhelming to plan time to get together, the relationship may feel one-sided to friends who find it easy to manage a full calendar and stay organized.

Since maintaining meaningful connections with others is essential to mental health, people with ADHD can benefit from practicing the skills needed to form and keep friendships. In one study, children and teenagers with ADHD participated in a fourteen-week program covering topics such as starting and carrying on conversations, using humor, practicing online etiquette, dealing with teasing or bullying, and hosting get-togethers. The participants completed a friendship-related homework assignment each week. By the end of the program, 70 percent of participants reported having made a new friend.

Dating and Marriage

The process of dating has many unspoken rules that people with ADHD may have trouble understanding and following. If you went on a date with someone who looked around while you were talking, changed the subject suddenly, fidgeted with clothes or jewelry constantly, or forgot something you just said, you would probably think that person was uninterested in you or maybe even rude. Yet these behaviors are common for people with ADHD. Often people with ADHD are unaware of how their actions are perceived.

Terena Bell, a freelance journalist, writes, "On a date I won't just notice you; I'll notice everything around you: the straw sticking out of our waiter's smock pocket, a flickering bulb in the light fixture, the wrinkles on the tablecloth. No matter how much I want to, I can't turn off the flood of stimuli and notice only you. Unless you know this, it's easy to think I'm not listening."[37]

People with ADHD also have to think about the right time to share their diagnosis. They might worry about getting too personal too quickly if they tell someone within the first couple of dates. On the other hand, they may worry that if they wait too long, the other person will be upset that it wasn't brought up sooner.

Impulsivity can be a particular risk when it comes to dating and sex. People with ADHD are at increased risk for sexually transmitted diseases and unwanted pregnancies. Managing impulsivity through the use of ADHD medication has proven effective in reducing risky sexual behaviors.

Relationship problems for people with ADHD don't disappear upon marriage. Once the excitement of dating is over, the reality of living with someone who has problems with organization, memory, and time management can put previously strong relationships to the test. Research shows that people with ADHD are nearly twice as likely to get divorced as the general population. The person who was once hyperfocused on his or her mate may seem distant and distractible at times. And frustration can build when a partner agrees to do a task but still hasn't done it hours later because he or she got distracted.

Melissa Orlov, a therapist who specializes in counseling couples dealing with ADHD, says both people must truly understand and accept what the condition means. "This acceptance can be difficult for both partners," she writes. "It's easier for an ADHD partner to say 'I've had ADHD all my life and done fine . . . my spouse's anger and frustration [are] the problem. And anyway, now I'm taking medication.'

Sleep Strategies

Ask people with ADHD if there's a single factor that makes the most difference in the severity of their symptoms, and many will offer the same response: sleep. Many people with ADHD have trouble winding down and shutting off their brains for the night. They may feel too restless to stay in bed, be bored by the lack of stimulation as they wait for sleep, or get distracted by worries and unfinished tasks. Not getting the quantity or quality of sleep they need can make it even more difficult to stay alert the next day. For many people, practicing "sleep hygiene" becomes part of their evening routine, much like putting on their pajamas and brushing their teeth. One key strategy involves having a consistent bedtime, ideally on weekends as well as weekdays. Another is doing a relaxing activity such as stretching, journaling, or meditating a half hour before bedtime. Sleeping in a dark and quiet room can also make a big difference, as can putting electronic devices away for the night to resist the urge to check texts or emails. While getting sufficient sleep is important for everyone, it is essential for people with ADHD. Adding fatigue to the challenge of paying attention makes daily living all the more difficult.

It's even easier for a non-ADHD partner . . . to point a finger at the ADHD partner and conclude 'There's something wrong with you, and you are the cause of all of our problems.'"[38] Orlov says blaming is what really harms marriage relationships. Each partner must take responsibility for his or her part in the dysfunction and commit to making changes. Writes Orlov,

> The ADHD partner needs to optimally treat the ADHD symptoms with physiological treatments such as medication and exercise, and then use the resulting improvements to change behavioral patterns. . . . The non-ADHD partner typically needs to lessen their desire to control the events in the relationship (and the behaviors of the ADHD partner), work on healing anger and trust issues, and reintroduce patience and empathy into their dealing with their spouse.[39]

Counseling can improve relationships, but it won't make ADHD disappear. Loving someone with ADHD means accepting that person for who he or she is—someone who possesses strengths and weaknesses just as everyone else does. And for the person with ADHD, love means making a commitment to manage the negative impact ADHD symptoms can have on an intimate relationship.

Parenting

Since ADHD is largely caused by genetic factors, some people with ADHD have children who also have the condition. Such parents, knowing the difficulties they have had in their own lives, may worry about whether they will be able to be good parents. Terry Matlen, a life coach who specializes in helping other mothers with ADHD, writes, "I wondered whether I had the parenting skills to raise [my daughter] well because of my ADHD. . . . If I couldn't keep my own workspace organized, how could I expect her to keep her bedroom and playroom in order? If I had problems with distractibility, how could I expect her to stay on task?"[40]

Parents with ADHD can be role models for their children by setting consistent rules and schedules, modeling coping strategies their

> "I wondered whether I had the parenting skills to raise [my daughter] well because of my ADHD. . . . If I couldn't keep my own workspace organized, how could I expect her to keep her bedroom and playroom in order? If I had problems with distractibility, how could I expect her to stay on task?"[40]
>
> —Terry Matlen, life coach

Parents who have a child with ADHD need to stay positive as they help their child learn life skills. The result will be a better outcome for everyone involved.

children can use, making sure their own symptoms are treated, and having compassion for themselves when they make mistakes. Matlen writes, "I burnt dinner, and forgot to bake brownies for [my daughter's] homeroom classmates. For a while, I beat myself up over it, but I learned to put my lapses in perspective. As years went by, whenever I'd screw up, I'd say, 'Guess my ADHD is kicking in again.'"[41]

A different array of challenges can result when parents who do not have ADHD have a child who does. When children with ADHD fall short in following directions, completing assigned tasks, or sitting still when asked to, strain in the parent-child relationship can result. Parents of children with ADHD need to acknowledge that their child may fail to meet their expectations not because the child is being disobedient or defiant but because she can't help it. One key to a healthy relationship is for parents to picture a bright future for their child despite the challenges ADHD can bring. Says parent Carol Barnier, "My child is destined for something wonderful, something that would be impossible for those calmer, regular-energy level children."[42]

Other strategies for successfully parenting a child with ADHD include being an effective advocate for the child, particularly at school. Some accommodations, including an IEP, may be needed in order for a child to do her best in school, and parents need to be proactive in speaking up for their child. Says psychology professor George DuPaul, "While it's true that your child's mind works differently, he certainly has the ability to learn and succeed just like any other kid. Look at it this way—if your child was diabetic or had asthma, would you, for one single minute, hesitate to advocate for his benefit?"[43] Other suggestions for establishing a healthy, productive parent-child relationship include making informed decisions about the use of medication, knowing the difference between discipline and punishment, anticipating potentially difficult situations, and avoiding negativity. School psychologist Sal Severe advises parents to "retrain

> "My child is destined for something wonderful, something that would be impossible for those calmer, regular-energy level children."[42]
>
> —Carol Barnier, parent of a child with ADHD

yourself to look at the positives. Catch your child being good or doing something well, and praise her. When you point out and praise desirable behaviors, you teach her what you want—not what you don't want."[44]

Managing Medication

ADHD medications are safe and effective when used properly, but not everyone takes them exactly as prescribed. Some people may forget to take their medication at the correct time, leading to "crashes" as the medication wears off. Children, in particular, require assistance in staying on a schedule. If a child is taking a short-acting form of medication, a dose may need to be administered during the school day to supplement what was taken at home. Timers and visual cues can be especially helpful in establishing a regular schedule. Podcast host Eric Tivers puts his pill bottle in his empty coffee cup each morning as a reminder to take the pill before having coffee.

Medications to treat ADHD also have a reputation for being intentionally misused. ADHD medications such as Adderall are popular "study drugs" on college campuses. Psychologist Ruth Hughes notes, "Some students who do not have ADHD may seek out stimulant medications with the belief that they may enhance their academic performance."[45] The thinking behind this belief is that if stimulant medications help a person with ADHD concentrate more intently, they will also help a neurotypical person in the same way. But scientists cast doubt on whether the medications bring much benefit to people without ADHD. Researcher Karen Miotto notes, "Research has shown that the placebo effect of ADHD drugs is quite large, so you feel more focused because you tell yourself that's supposed to be the effect."[46]

As controlled substances, ADHD medications should only be taken if prescribed by a doctor. Abusing these drugs is dangerous and illegal.

In addition to the drugs frequently not having their intended effect, abuse of controlled substances can bring serious legal consequences. Says student affairs administrator Kevin Kruger, "Often, students who inappropriately use ADHD prescription medications don't realize the consequences it may have on their academic career and future livelihood."[47] In an interview with CNN, an anonymous student who obtains ADHD medication without a prescription stated, "The fact that it's illegal really doesn't cross my mind. It's not something that I get nervous about because it's so widespread and simple."[48]

Because ADHD medications are often seen as desirable, people with ADHD may feel pressured by friends, coworkers, or partners to share their medication. Doing so is dangerous. Misuse of stimulants can put extreme strain on the heart and circulatory system. Excessive doses can cause panic attacks and psychosis. Combined with alcohol, which is a depressant, stimulants can even be deadly. Furthermore, many prescribed and over-the-counter medicines interact with ADHD medication, making the combination life-threatening for people with certain medical conditions. People with ADHD should set clear boundaries about their medication and rethink any relationships in which they are pressured to share it.

Chapter 4

ADHD TREATMENT

For many people, finding the right ADHD treatment is the difference between thriving in school, work, or relationships and struggling to get through each day. Ways of treating ADHD can be broadly divided into three categories: medication, talk-based therapy, and supportive treatments.

Medication

Medications have been widely used to treat ADHD since the 1960s. Several stimulants commonly used to treat ADHD are known commercially as Ritalin, Adderall, Concerta, and Vyvanse. At first glance, it is surprising that a stimulant would effectively treat hyperactivity. Researchers explain this seeming contradiction by noting that hyperactive symptoms may reflect the presence of too much dopamine in the basal ganglia portion of the brain. The cluster of neurons known as the basal ganglia is primarily responsible for one's motor control. When a person with ADHD takes a stimulant, dopamine activity decreases in the basal ganglia and increases in the prefrontal cortex, the portion of the brain that controls cognition and decision-making.

Unlike antidepressant medications, which can take weeks to have an effect, stimulants work within approximately thirty to sixty minutes of taking the first dose. They also wear off quickly, so some people take extended-release capsules that deliver timed doses throughout the day. There are also several nonstimulant medications used to treat ADHD, such as Strattera and Intuniv. These medications work by increasing levels of norepinephrine and epinephrine, two neurochemicals that also affect mood, attention, and energy.

Many people say that finding the right medication is life-changing. Michelle Beckett, who was diagnosed with ADHD as an adult, describes it this way: "Life felt so much easier on medication. No longer the constant motorway of thoughts and ideas at such speed, but calm stillness. I was still me, full of enthusiastic ideas and a feisty spark to change the world, but a healthier version. Like a car that previously spluttered through life with an engine problem but was now mostly fixed."[49]

The downside to medications is that the increase in dopamine

> **"Life felt so much easier on medication. No longer the constant motorway of thoughts and ideas at such speed, but calm stillness. I was still me, full of enthusiastic ideas and a feisty spark to change the world, but a healthier version."[49]**
>
> —Michelle Beckett, diagnosed with ADHD as an adult

and norepinephrine in the brain can cause unwelcome side effects. These include anxiety, increased heart rate, stomachaches, loss of appetite, and sleep problems. Some people also feel medication changes their personality in ways they don't like. Rachel Cassandra, who started taking ADHD medication at age twelve and chose to stop it as an adult, writes, "Medication interferes with both my creativity and the identification of my true interests. It has allowed me to focus on anything, inherently reducing the pull of those topics I find truly compelling—like fiction writing, like art, the things on which I hyper focus."[50] Adds Cassandra, now a freelance writer, "I still lose track of my notebooks and drift during conversations with others. I lose water bottles at a rapid clip and have trouble sitting through an entire movie. Though I try to adapt to the world, these traits and tendencies are a fundamental part of me, not something I'd like to erase [any more] than I would the freckles on my shoulders or my angular nose."[51]

> "Though I try to adapt to the world, these traits and tendencies are a fundamental part of me, not something I'd like to erase [any more] than I would the freckles on my shoulders or my angular nose."[51]
>
> —Rachel Cassandra, former user of ADHD medication

When a child has ADHD, parents must decide whether or not to have the child take medication. Some parents are concerned about side effects, including the medications' potential impact on growth. Because stimulants can reduce one's appetite, children who use them may take in fewer calories and nutrients than they normally would. This can result in suppressed growth in height and weight. But the overall evidence suggests that stimulants do not have a long-term impact on growth. For some parents, the solution to this concern is to have their children take "medication holidays" on weekends or vacations when there is less need for focused attention. Research indicates that discontinuing treatment for an entire summer allows children to make up for any growth suppression that may have occurred while taking stimulants during the school year.

Parents also worry about whether their child could become dependent on medication or could become more likely to abuse drugs in the future. While it is true that some ADHD medications are amphetamines, a class of drugs that can be very addictive, dependence occurs only at very high doses and typically when not taken orally, such as by injection. There is no evidence that ADHD medication causes addiction when taken as prescribed. And while children and teens with ADHD are at higher risk for future substance abuse than are children and teens in general, their greater risk comes from behavioral tendencies associated with ADHD, not from the use of therapeutic medication. The three main ADHD symptoms of inattention, impulsivity, and hyperactivity can cause problems at home, in school, and in social settings that may predispose a young person to abuse drugs or alcohol. Some experts even assert that appropriate use of medication to regulate behavior makes people with ADHD less likely to become substance abusers than they would be without medication. In particular, physician Timothy Wilens writes, "Studies show that adolescents with ADHD who respond well to their medications are at lower risk for substance abuse compared [to] those who respond poorly to their medication."[52]

STIMULANT EFFECTS

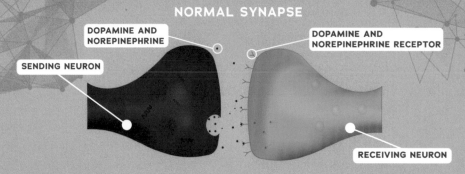

NORMAL SYNAPSE

DOPAMINE AND NOREPINEPHRINE

DOPAMINE AND NOREPINEPHRINE RECEPTOR

SENDING NEURON

RECEIVING NEURON

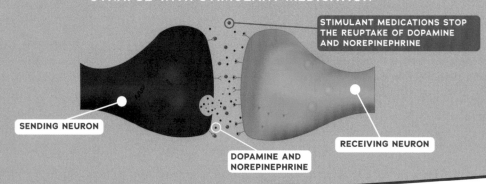

SYNAPSE WITH STIMULANT MEDICATION

STIMULANT MEDICATIONS STOP THE REUPTAKE OF DOPAMINE AND NOREPINEPHRINE

SENDING NEURON

RECEIVING NEURON

DOPAMINE AND NOREPINEPHRINE

Neurons are electrically charged cells that transmit information through chemical messaging. The average human brain contains approximately 100 billion neurons. To convey a message, the sending side of a neuron transmits an electrical impulse across the space known as the synapse. Neurochemicals such as dopamine and norepinephrine aid in the transport of these electrical signals. Stimulant medications used to treat ADHD increase available levels of these neurotransmitters. They do so by preventing the reabsorption, or reuptake, of these chemicals on the sending side of a nerve transmission, leading to a greater concentration in the synaptic space. This higher concentration means more of the chemicals can be absorbed on the receiving side. Maintaining these elevated levels can strengthen the brain's ability to regulate attention and impulsivity, among other effects.

Many studies show that people have short-term improvement in symptoms when they take ADHD medications. The evidence for their long-term effects is less clear, because it is difficult to maintain contact with study participants over the course of years or decades. In addition, it is very challenging to obtain accurate information about study participants' medication use during such a long period. For many people with ADHD, any concerns they have about using ADHD medication to manage their symptoms are offset by the negative effects of not using them.

Therapy for ADHD

Talk-based therapies of various kinds are the second most common treatment for ADHD. In an article for *ADDitude* magazine, teacher Anne Dykstra writes, "Counseling was the key to helping me realize that I could survive and live with ADHD. Without counseling, I would have never graduated college to become a teacher."[53] In the same article, Matt [last name withheld] writes, "[Counseling] was crucial in helping me realize that I had to re-learn behaviors that I had been compensating for during the years of being untreated."[54]

Therapy can be undertaken alone or in combination with medication. In addition to seeking ways to manage their symptoms, clients might discuss problems that can be caused by ADHD, such as low self-esteem or

"Counseling was the key to helping me realize that I could survive and live with ADHD. Without counseling, I would have never graduated college to become a teacher."[53]

—Anne Dykstra, teacher

Disorder or Difference?

Some people do not believe ADHD is a disorder at all. Instead, they believe the condition is a normal variation in brain function that occurs within the population. Those who hold this view are part of the neurodiversity movement. People in this movement advocate for the rights of those who have ADHD, autism, dyslexia, and other neurological conditions. In an article for *Psychology Today*, neuroscientist Marc Lewis writes, "Many scientists believe that a certain amount of psychological diversity is built into the human race because it provides an evolutionary advantage for all of us." Thus, people with ADHD may benefit society by having a greater capacity for creative problem-solving than do "neurotypical" people, for example.

Supporters of the neurodiversity movement argue that people with these conditions do not need to change just to meet society's expectations; rather, society should change to better accommodate their different ways of thinking and acting. Opponents of the neurodiversity movement argue that normalizing these conditions prevents people from seeking treatment, leading to unnecessary hardship.

Most mental health professionals take a balanced approach. They treat symptoms that impair their clients' ability to function in daily life, but they also encourage schools and workplaces to be more accepting of differences, and they help their clients secure accommodations when needed.

Marc Lewis, "Disease, Disorder, or Neurodiversity: The Case of ADHD," *Psychology Today*, May 21, 2012. www.psychologytoday.com.

relationship difficulties. Because therapy addresses the whole person, it can help people with ADHD who also struggle with substance abuse, depression, anxiety, eating disorders, and other mental health conditions. Talk-based therapy comes in many varieties, and several types seem to be particularly helpful for people with ADHD.

Behavior Therapy

Behavior therapy is a system of using positive and negative feedback to shape a person's actions. Positive reinforcement involves a reward, such as verbal praise or stars on a chart, that has the effect of increasing a desired behavior. Negative reinforcement involves avoiding something undesirable, such as a parent's yelling, that then increases a desired behavior. A behavior therapist working with Aidan, for example, might create a reward system to curb his impulsive behavior. Because behavior therapy has few risks and many proven benefits, the American Academy of Pediatrics recommends that parents try behavior therapy before medication for preschool-aged children with ADHD.

Cognitive Behavioral Therapy

Another talk therapy for ADHD involves reshaping ways of thinking. Cognitive behavioral therapy (CBT) requires that people have a fairly high level of awareness about their thoughts and feelings, as well as the ability to express them in words. For this reason, it is most commonly used for older children, teens, and adults. In CBT, people learn to identify automatic thoughts that trigger certain behaviors, and to replace them with new, more productive thoughts. For example, Tori might think, "I can't believe I screwed up again!" in response to forgetting a meeting. A CBT therapist might help Tori come up with a more neutral way of thinking.

Family Therapy

ADHD affects not only the people who have the condition, but everyone close to them. In family therapy, the parents, spouses, siblings, or children of the person with ADHD also attend sessions. The goal is to identify unhelpful patterns between family members and create new ways of understanding and relating.

For example, if Olivia attended a family therapy session, she might be what is called the "identified patient"—the person whose behavior

Trained counselors can suggest practical solutions to common challenges faced by people with ADHD. They can help a patient change his or her own behavior over time.

was the reason the family sought assistance. Olivia's father might say he always has to nag her to do her chores and clean up her room. Olivia might say her father is too critical and that he calls her hurtful names such as "space cadet." A family therapist would help them develop more positive ways of interacting. Over time, family members learn to communicate their needs and feelings to each other without a therapist as a go-between.

Narrative Therapy

The stories people tell about themselves to themselves can shape their lives for better or worse. Narrative therapists focus on listening to the stories of people with an illness or disability, helping them rewrite new, more positive ways of thinking about themselves. Peggy Derivan, who practices this type of therapy, writes:

> Narrative therapists . . . help people identify alternative stories that are wider in scope and integrate relevant facts about the person's strengths that might not be identified in a narrower version of the story. The alternative story allows people to place more emphasis on their hopes, abilities, values, beliefs, desires, and commitments, and begin to live life in the context of these preferred ideas and experiences.[55]

A narrative therapist would not focus explicitly on changing someone's behavior. For example, if Aidan forgets to turn in his homework all week, a narrative therapist would probably not focus on that situation. Instead, she might seek an "alternative story" of a time when Aidan did finish his homework. How was that day different? What did he do when he started to get distracted? What could he do to have more days like that?

Narrative therapists also use a technique called externalizing. This turns the label *ADHD* from something the person is to something the person has. The therapist might use language

"Narrative therapists . . . help people identify alternative stories that are wider in scope and integrate relevant facts about the person's strengths that might not be identified in a narrower version of the story. The alternative story allows people to place more emphasis on their hopes, abilities, values, beliefs, desires, and commitments, and begin to live life in the context of these preferred ideas and experiences."[55]

—Peggy Derivan, narrative therapist

like, "It sounds like your ADHD was running the show at school today" instead of "It sounds like you weren't listening to your teacher today." Narrative therapy can be a creative way of helping people rewrite the story of their ADHD.

Client-Centered and Integrative Therapy

Often, when people see a therapist, the session may be less structured than the approaches described above. It might look more like a conversation in which the therapist asks open-ended questions, explores what the client is feeling, and offers insights into the situation. This is called client-centered counseling, and it is what many people think of when they imagine therapy. The clinician might also use an integrative approach, in which she uses techniques from different types of therapy that she feels would be helpful to the client. This is a common way of working with adults and older adolescents who may prefer sessions with less structure and more freedom to discuss their thoughts, feelings, and experiences in the moment. Good therapists will listen carefully for the heartfelt concerns and struggles likely to be expressed by a person with ADHD.

Supportive Treatments

Beyond medication and talk-based therapy, there are a variety of other treatments that may help people with ADHD. These supportive treatments have less evidence-based support, but there are many individual accounts of people who have found them helpful. One of these is coaching. Coaching for mental health looks similar to therapy, but it has a few key differences. While therapy tends to process deeper emotional issues, coaching is more informal and tends to involve a specific goal, such as getting to work on time, establishing a workout schedule, or preparing a presentation. Coaches do not have to be licensed mental health professionals, although many have degrees in social work or psychology. One advantage to coaching over traditional therapy is that it can be done by telephone. Says ADHD coach Sarah Wright, "Telephone coaching is time-effective . . . and it's discreet. If you don't want your colleagues to know about your ADHD, you can talk with a coach on your cell phone in your car during lunch, and go back to your office when the session is over."[56]

Coaching tends to be appropriate for people with fairly straightforward difficulties, such as a student seeking to practice better study habits or an employee wanting to be more organized at work. Someone with more severe ADHD who might be failing multiple subjects and struggling socially would probably need the added support of therapy and medication.

Mindfulness is the practice of bringing one's experience to the present moment. One of the best-known modern mindfulness researchers, Jon Kabat-Zinn, defines mindfulness this way: "Mindfulness is awareness that arises through paying attention, on purpose, in the present moment, non-judgmentally. It's about knowing what is on your mind."[57]

Practicing focused attention can be particularly helpful for people with ADHD. When people practice mindfulness, they are more likely to notice when their attention strays from a task. For example, a student might realize he has spent the last hour watching videos of puppies on YouTube instead of writing a history paper as he intended. Mindfulness will allow him to calmly return his attention to the task at hand without mentally beating himself up or thinking his whole day has been a waste.

There are different ways to practice mindfulness. Some people practice a formal, sitting-style mindfulness in which a class instructor or a recording guides their thinking for thirty minutes. Others practice mindfulness while walking their dogs, drinking a cup of hot chocolate, or playing baseball. People with ADHD often feel their attention and activity is outside of their control. But in one study, 78 percent of participants who practiced mindfulness felt their ADHD symptoms improved. Lidia Zylowska, a psychiatrist who specializes in mindfulness, writes, "Typically when we first practice mindfulness, we find how really busy our mind is . . . . With more practice, or with more intense relaxation, we may experience some quieting of the mind."[58]

> "Typically when we first practice mindfulness, we find how really busy our mind is . . . . With more practice, or with more intense relaxation, we may experience some quieting of the mind."[58]
>
> —Psychiatrist Lidia Zylowska

Exercise, Diet, and Nutrition

For people with ADHD, being forced to sit still for too long can feel almost like torture. Getting regular activity can be part of the solution, as exercise reduces both hyperactive and inattentive symptoms. This may be because exercise releases dopamine and other neurochemicals in the areas of the brain that are underactive in people with ADHD. One study of children with ADHD found that horseback riding improved motor skills, social interactions, and quality of life. Since people with ADHD tend to be highly motivated to do things they enjoy, practicing a sport or activity they find fun and exciting is key.

Some people with ADHD turn to specific diets or supplements that are supposed to improve focus or reduce hyperactivity. So far, there is not a lot of evidence in this area. A 2007 study in the United Kingdom found that certain artificial food colorings were associated with symptoms of hyperactivity in children. In other studies, findings about the benefits of fish oil in improving mood and concentration have been mixed.

Specific diets for ADHD are often based on cutting out certain food categories or components, such as dairy and gluten. These are known to trigger allergic or immune system reactions in some people, which can affect mood and behavior. Although some people with ADHD have reported improvement in their symptoms after following such diets, no controlled research studies have examined the issue.

Neurofeedback

Neurofeedback is a somewhat controversial treatment for ADHD. In this method, the patient puts on a tight-fitting cap that measures electrical activity in the brain. He then sees a visual recording of his brainwave patterns and learns about the mental states associated with each of them. For example, delta waves are associated with sleep. If these waves are present while the patient is awake, they may indicate a lack of focused attention. Beta waves, in contrast, indicate a focused, alert state, ideal for work and study. By receiving real-time feedback about his brainwaves, the person hooked up to the EEG learns how to create specific types of brainwaves on purpose.

Research on neurofeedback is mixed. One study found a neurofeedback program to be nearly as effective as group CBT, but many clinicians find fault with the way the study was conducted. Interestingly, this same study showed that a fake neurofeedback treatment—where patients were hooked up to an EEG machine that was not actually measuring their brainwaves—was nearly as effective as both real neurofeedback and CBT treatment. This illustrates the power of the placebo effect, in which people who believe a treatment will help them experience real improvement. At this time, there are no official guidelines for using neurofeedback to treat ADHD. For this reason, many clinicians do not recommend it.

Because there is no "one-size-fits-all" approach to treating ADHD, people may have to experiment with several types of treatment, in different doses and combinations, before they see results. But the effort is worthwhile—about 80 percent of people who seek treatment for ADHD notice significant improvement.

Bicycle Brakes

After working with thousands of patients who have ADHD, psychiatrist Edward Hallowell developed a creative way of informing his young patients that they have ADHD:

> *After putting all [the testing] information together, I'm now able to tell you that you have an awesome brain. Your brain is very powerful. It's like a Ferrari—a race car. You have the power to win races and become a champion. However, you do have one problem. You have bicycle brakes. Your brakes just aren't strong enough to control your powerful brain, so you can't slow down or stop when you need to. Your mind goes off wherever it wants*

Physical activities bring a variety of benefits to children and adults with ADHD. Sports not only help people stay healthy, but they can also improve ADHD symptoms.

to go, instead of staying on track. But not to worry! I'm a brake specialist, and if you work with me, we can strengthen your brakes.[59]

Hallowell appropriately recognizes both the challenges and opportunities that come with ADHD. As with any health condition, living with ADHD requires proactive management and creative problem-solving. Since ADHD affects all aspects of a person's life, including education, job performance, and family and social relationships, it is essential to find strategies that manage symptoms effectively. With appropriate treatment, social support, self-knowledge, and self-compassion, people with ADHD can channel their unique way of thinking and behaving into building a rewarding, productive life.

SOURCE NOTES

INTRODUCTION: THREE FACES OF ADHD

1. "Understanding ADHD—the Basics," *WebMD,* n.d. www.webmd.com.

2. National Institute of Mental Health, *Attention Deficit Hyperactivity Disorder,* March 2016. www.nimh.gov.

3. *ADDitude* editors, Devon Frye, and Larry Silver, "Is Attention Deficit Disorder (ADHD/ADD) Hereditary? Yes and No," *ADDitude,* n.d. www.additudemag.com.

4. CHADD, "The Science of ADHD," 2018. www.chadd.org.

5. *ADHD Boss* Editorial Team, "The History of ADHD—Past Mistakes, Present Knowledge & Future Hope," *ADHD Boss,* July 29, 2017. www.adhdboss.com.

CHAPTER 1: WHAT IS ADHD?

6. Blake Taylor, *ADHD and Me: What I Learned from Lighting Fires at the Dinner Table.* Oakland, CA: New Harbinger, 2008, p. 87.

7. Quoted in Rafi Letzter, "What It's Like to Live with ADHD So Severe It Feels Like 'Brain Fog,'" *Business Insider,* May 29, 2017. www.businessinsider.com.

8. Quoted in Melissa McGlensey, "18 People Explain What ADHD Feels Like," *The Mighty,* February 26, 2016. themighty.com.

9. Quoted in McGlensey, "18 People Explain What ADHD Feels Like."

10. Anna Selleck, "ADHD: How to Survive with a Wild Child," *Guardian,* May 28, 2010. www.theguardian.com.

11. Quoted in R. Morgan Griffin, "Sharing a Diagnosis: When You and Your Child Have ADHD," *WebMD,* September 4, 2008. www.webmd.com.

12. Quoted in Tammy Murphy, "His Energy Drains Me," *ADDitude,* Fall 2011. www.additudemag.com.

13. Jessica McCabe, "What the Ups and Downs of ADHD in a Day Can Look Like," *Healthline,* July 27, 2017. www.healthline.com.

14. *ADDitude,* "ADHD, By the Numbers," n.d. www.additudemag.com.

15. McCabe, "What the Ups and Downs of ADHD in a Day Can Look Like."

16. Quoted in Denise Foley, "Growing Up with ADHD," *Time,* n.d., time.com.

17. Kathleen O'Brien, "'But You're Too Smart to Have ADHD,'" *The Mighty,* September 4, 2016. themighty.com.

18. Quoted in Carl Sherman, "Coping with the Stigma of ADHD," *ADDitude,* April/May 2007. www.additudemag.com.

19. Rebecca Winchell, "Let's Talk about Hyperfocus," *The Mighty,* October 21, 2016. themighty.com.

20. Quoted in Patricia Sellers, "JetBlue Founder Speaks Out about His ADD," *Fortune,* June 12, 2008. fortune.com.

21. Quoted in Sellers, "JetBlue Founder Speaks Out."

22. Edward Hallowell, "ADHD Overview: Top 10 Questions on ADHD," *Live a Better Life,* n.d. www.drhallowell.com.

CHAPTER 2: ADHD SYMPTOMS AND DIAGNOSIS

23. Klaus W. Lange et al., "The History of Attention Deficit Hyperactivity Disorder," *NCBI,* November 30, 2010. www.ncbi.nlm.nih.gov.

24. Quoted in WBUR News, "'Paying Attention' with an ADHD Mother and Son," October 7, 2010. www.bur.org.

25. Larry Silver, "Boys with ADHD Need Their Dads," *ADDitude,* n.d. www.additudemag.com.

26. Quoted in Matt McMillen, "How Sports Can Help Kids with ADHD," *WebMD,* August 25, 2014. www.webmd.com.

27. Quoted in *ADDitude*, "What Was Your Reaction to Your Child's Diagnosis?" n.d. www.additudemag.com.

28. Quoted in *ADDitude*, "What Was Your Reaction to Your Child's Diagnosis?"

29. Quoted in *ADDitude*, "What Was Your Reaction to Your Child's Diagnosis?"

30. Quoted in *ADDitude*, "What Was Your Reaction to Your Child's Diagnosis?"

31. Quoted in *ADDitude*, "What Was Your Reaction to Your Child's Diagnosis?"

32. Michelle Beckett, "The Day I Almost Died—But Instead Found Hope," *ADDitude*, n.d. www.additudemag.com.

CHAPTER 3: LIVING WITH ADHD

33. Quoted in Terena Bell, "Don't Tell Your Boss You Have ADHD," *Tonic*, May 3, 2017. tonic.vice.com.

34. Beth Main, "I Want to Stop Forgetting Things!" *ADDitude*, n.d. www.additudemag.com.

35. Quoted in Patricia Berry, "Where's the Passion?" *ADDitude*, n.d. www.additudemag.com.

36. Foley, "Growing Up with ADHD."

37. Terena Bell, "Dating with ADHD: When Do I Tell a New Partner about My Health Condition?" *Washington Post*, December 11, 2017. www.washingtonpost.com.

38. Melissa Orlov, "ADHD Doesn't Cause Divorce, Denial Does," *Psychology Today*, September 18, 2013. www.psychologytoday.com.

39. Orlov, "ADHD Doesn't Cause Divorce."

40. Terry Matlen, "Mom Guilt Is Destructive. Here's How to Ditch It," *ADDitude*, n.d. www.additudemag.com.

41. Matlen, "Mom Guilt is Destructive."

42. Quoted in Deborah Carpenter, "Never Punish a Child for Behavior Outside His Control," *ADDitude*, June/July 2006. www.additudemag.com.

43. Carpenter, "Never Punish a Child for Behavior Outside His Control."

44. Carpenter, "Never Punish a Child for Behavior Outside His Control."

45. Quoted in PR Newswire, *New Coalition Aims to Help Prevent Misuse, Abuse and Diversion of ADHD Medications*, August 28, 2014. www.prnewswire.com.

46. Quoted in Maggie Puniewska, "What Are the Effects of Adderall if You Don't Have ADHD?" *Tonic,* November 18, 2016. tonic.vice.com.

47. Quoted in PR Newswire, *New Coalition Aims to Help Prevent Misuse, Abuse and Diversion of ADHD Medications.*

48. Quoted in Arianna Yanes, "Just Say Yes? The Rise of 'Study Drugs' in College," *CNN,* April 18, 2014. www.cnn.com.

CHAPTER 4: ADHD TREATMENT

49. Beckett, "The Day I Almost Died."

50. Rachel Cassandra, "Why I Stopped Taking My ADD Pills," *Tonic,* June 1, 2016, tonic.vice.com.

51. Cassandra, "Why I Stopped Taking My ADD Pills."

52. Timothy Wilens, "Does Stimulant Medication Cause Addiction?" *ADDitude,* n.d. www.additudemag.com.

53. Quoted in *ADDitude*, "Therapy Helped Me . . .," Spring 2010. www.additudemag.com.

54. Quoted in *ADDitude*, "Therapy Helped Me . . ."

55. Peggy Derivan, "Overcoming Tough Problems with Kids: A Narrative Therapist's Approach," *Discoveries Counseling,* June 11, 2015. discoveries-counseling.com.

56. Quoted in Laura Flynn McCarthy, "What If You Could Hire a Life-with-ADHD Coach?" *ADDitude,* n.d. www.additudemag.com.

57. Quoted in Mindful, *Jon Kabat-Zinn: Defining Mindfulness,* January 11, 2017. www.mindful.org.

58. Quoted in Stephanie Sarkis, "ADHD & Mindfulness: An Interview with Lidia Zylowska MD," *Psychology Today,* June 19, 2012. www.psychologytoday.com.

59. Edward Hallowell, "Ferrari Engines, Bicycle Brakes," *ASCD Educational Leadership,* October 2012. www.ascd.org.

BOOKS

Thomas E. Brown, *Smart but Stuck: Emotions in Teens and Adults with ADHD*. San Francisco: Jossey-Bass, 2014.

Debra E. Burdick, *Mindfulness for Teens with ADHD: A Skill-Building Workbook to Help You Focus & Succeed*. Oakland, CA: Instant Help Books, 2017.

Edward M. Hallowell and John J. Ratey. *Driven to Distraction: Recognizing and Coping with Attention Deficit Disorder from Childhood Through Adulthood*. New York: Anchor Books, 2011.

Ruth Spodak and Kenneth Stefano. *Take Control of ADHD: The Ultimate Guide for Teens with ADHD*. Waco, TX: Prufrock Press, 2011.

Blake Taylor. *ADHD and Me: What I Learned from Lighting Fires at the Dinner Table*. Oakland, CA: New Harbinger, 2007.

INTERNET SOURCES

Angela Aguirre, "Not Just LIVING but THRIVING with ADHD." *TedXCalStateLA*, June 8, 2017. www.youtube.com.

Karen Barrow, "Patient Voices: A.D.H.D," *New York Times*. May 2008. www.nytimes.com.

Bonnie Berkowitz and Patterson Clark, "Your Brain on ADHD." *Washington Post*. June 1, 2015. www.washingtonpost.com.

WEBSITES

ADDitude Magazine
www.additudemag.com

The website for *ADDitude* magazine is a resource for families and adults living with ADHD, covering a wide range of topics.

ADDYTeen
www.addyteen.com

ADDYTeen is a community-support website for teens created by Grace Friedman, a teen with ADHD. The site also offers resources and information for parents and counselors.

ADHD reWired
www.adhdrewired.com

ADHD reWired is a website initiated by licensed social worker Eric Tivers. The site features a podcast in which Tivers interviews guests who have ADHD, as well as some who discuss recent research. Site users can join an online coaching group as well as a private Facebook group.

CHADD
www.chadd.org

CHADD (Children and Adults with Attention-Deficit/Hyperactivity Disorder) is a national membership organization for people with ADHD. CHADD provides education, advocacy, and support for people with ADHD. The website serves as a clearinghouse of ADHD information.

The Mighty
themighty.com

The Mighty is an online community that connects people facing health challenges and disabilities. The site consists of first-person accounts and articles by people living with a variety of physical and mental health conditions.

IMAGE CREDITS

Whitney Sanderson is a writer in Massachusetts. She is the author of numerous fiction and nonfiction books for young readers. She has a master's degree in clinical psychology from Bridgewater State University, with a special interest in narrative therapy. She also lives with ADHD.